THE POWER OF RE

BY KRISTIN REEG

DEDICATION

This book is dedicated to everyone who ever struggled to understand a definition or a Christian concept.

ACKNOWLEDGMENTS

First and foremost, I'd like to thank my Heavenly Father, Jesus Christ, and Holy Spirit. Without the love, forgiveness, and healing I have received from them, I would not be who I am today.

I would like to thank my editor and mother, Sandra Reeg. Thank you for believing in me and in this project. Your input, minor corrections, and encouragement are priceless.

Jeana Borkholder, you're amazing! Without you I'm not sure this book would be in existence. You are a treasured gem in my life.

Tina Croft, God has blessed me greatly with your friendship. Thank you for helping me process my thoughts, encouraging me to grow, and loving me through my dark season.

Also, I want to extend my gratitude to my social media family. Thank you for the likes, the loves, and the comments that encouraged me to "press on" with this unusual manuscript.

KRISTIN REEG

Table of Contents

INTRODUCTION

Have you ever noticed how many words begin with the letters "RE"? As if being spoken through a megaphone, these words have been echoing in my ears. According to most English dictionaries, there are more than 4,000 words that start with the letters RE.

As I was praying with a dear friend, I felt impressed to write an entire devotional devoted to words often used in Christian circles that begin with RE. Throughout the following pages, I have provided the definition of 30 words using various dictionaries. With each word, my hope is to share the Father's heart through revelation, inspiration, and motivation.

For those of you, who like me love to alphabetize things, I ask for your forgiveness. You will not find the words in alphabetical order. (I tried!) As I began to format the book, I felt a strong urge to simply share the words in the order in which they were given. This book has a progression to it; therefore, to alphabetize would interrupt the journey.

This book isn't only about learning the meaning of words. It's a journey back to the heartbeat of Jesus. It's a relearning of things we may think we already know, but may have forgotten, or have been twisted by the trials of life. Let's get back to the basics. Let's seek to know the truth and allow it to sink into our souls to experience freedom as Jesus promised.

You are greatly loved! May you find restoration, revelation, rejuvenation, and redemption throughout the pages of this book.

1. RESTORE

RESTORE. The Lord has been speaking a lot about restoration. What in your life would you like to see restored? What has the enemy stolen from you that you want back? Is it a relationship? Your health? Your finances? Or is it something intangible? Your confidence? Your dignity? Your worth?

God cares about what you care about. There is evidence in the Bible of health being restored, money restored, possessions restored, land restored. Jesus is the very embodiment of restoration; He came to restore the relationship between humans and their Creator.

Maybe what we all really need is a restoration of our belief that God is good. Maybe life and the tyranny of the urgent have pulled us away from a belief that God is truly for us. Maybe our good deeds without reward have caused weariness to settle deep in our hearts. Perhaps what we need restored more than anything is the simple belief and faith that God is good.

King David said, "I remain confident of this: I will see the goodness of the LORD in the land of the living" (Psalm 27:13 NIV).

Whatever it is that we need God to restore in our lives, let's begin by believing that He is not only capable, but willing. Let's stretch our faith. Let's ask the Lord if there is anything we need to do to bring about the desired results. If so, then let's commit to taking the first steps. We are co-labors with Christ. When we take one step, God will take 10.

2. REUNION

REUNION

webstersdictionary1828.com

1. A second union; union formed anew after separation or discord;

2. In medicine, union of parts separated by wounds or accidents.

KRISTINREEG.COM #THEPOWEROFRE

Our general concept of reunion is a once a year gathering of extended family members at a park or picnic. But what if it's much more than that? What if reunion is actually taking something that was broken and putting it back together? What if it was finding parts of yourself that you thought were lost and bringing them back into the forefront? What if reunion was more related to healing than eating?

Lord, would You open our hearts to reunite us with the parts of us that wound or accidents have kept hidden? Would you come defragment our souls and enable a glorious reunion of who we were created to be? Father, to the wounded/ bruised areas of our souls, we choose to forgive those who have hurt us. We forgive people for misunderstanding us and not loving us the way we need to be loved. Forgive us, God, for misunderstanding others and not loving them the way they need to be loved. Unity is the cry of Your heart, God! Would You release a spirit of reunion and bring healing and restoration to fractured relationships? Awaken our hearts to hear Your voice, to recognize Your guidance, and to be reunited with You in spirit and in truth. In Jesus name. Amen.

3. RECOMPENSE

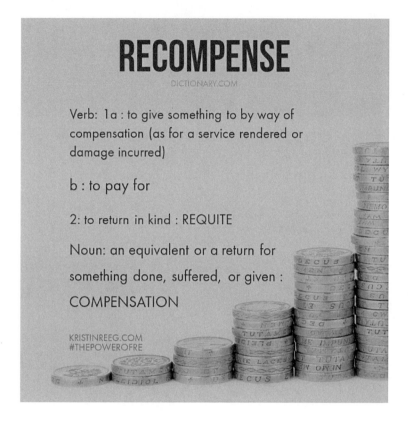

Many modern prophets of the Lord have been saying that God is decreeing a season of recompense. We can get so excited over a concept but have no idea what it actually means. So let this sink in: God is going to make the enemy compensate you for all the suffering and damage you have incurred!

While I do believe that this is largely related to finances, I also believe that there will be a time for extreme grace in relationships. The enemy will be forced to give you a reprieve from attacks on your relationships. This reprieve will open doors for restoration and recompense. Your relationships will grow and deepen at accelerated rates.

There has been so much warfare and pruning in the last couple of years that it can be difficult to tell the difference. If God pruned you, it was to grow you. If the enemy fought you, it was to destroy you. If you're still in the battle, lift your sword and shield again! Let the enemy know that though he may have wearied you, he has not overcome you. You will not be defeated; the Angel of the Lord is fighting on your behalf. You will obtain victory! And when you do: RECOMPENSE! That slithering snake will be forced to repay and compensate you for all the damages you incurred- emotionally, physically, and financially! So, rise up mighty warrior! The battle belongs to the Lord! (1 Samuel 17:47 NIV)

4. REJUVENATE

REJUVENATE

MERRIAM-WEBSTER.COM

1a : to make young or youthful again : give new vigor to

b : to restore to an original or new state

2a : to stimulate (a stream) to renewed erosive activity especially by uplift

b : to develop youthful features of topography in

KRISTINREEG.COM #THEPOWEROFRE

God wants to rejuvenate you! Some of you have been so wearied from the battle that it's been a stretch just to get out of bed in the morning! Not only has your physical body taken hits during the war, but your spirit and soul are also exhausted.

I hear the spirit of the Lord saying that He there is a revival coming to your energy levels! Those who wait upon the Lord SHALL renew their strength! They will mount up with wings like eagles. They shall run and not be weary. They will walk and not grow faint (Isaiah 40:31). There is fresh vigor, energy, and excitement coming to your soul! Those areas that have become numb from the intensity of the battle are going to feel again! God is going to renew your strength! You are going to feel like living again! You are going to feel alive again!

Holy Spirit, we invite You to come and rejuvenate our bodies, souls, and spirits! Ignite a fresh fire within us, like the fire in the altar that never goes out! Bring us back to childlike faith. Enable us to see our battles and what You are doing in our lives from a fresh perspective. Restore our joy! Help us to know that we have the freedom to laugh – and laugh loudly! Strengthen us and protect our hearts through the power of Your joy within us! Let us laugh and dance and raise the flags! Rejuvenate every area within us that has grown weary. You are good! Release a mighty wind to blow off the dead branches that the locusts and the cankerworms have eaten. Let us start afresh – renewed, invigorated, and rejuvenated in Jesus name!

5. RENEW

RENEW

DICTIONARY.COM

1. resume (an activity) after an interruption.

2. re-establish

3. repeat (an action or statement).

4. give fresh life or strength to

5. extend for a further period a validity of

6. replace (something that is broken or worn out)

KRISTINREEG.COM #THEPOWEROFRE

In Romans 12, Paul exhorts us to renew our minds daily! "Do not allow this world to mold you in its own image. Instead, be transformed from the inside out by renewing your mind. As a result, you will be able to discern what God wills and whatever God finds good, pleasing, and complete," (Romans 12:2 Voice).

The concept of renewing is much more than simply refreshing something. One of the definitions is to replace. It's time to renew our minds daily! It's time to replace religious traditions that have been broken or worn out with the actual word of God. It's time to replace the lies of the enemy and the incorrect perceptions of God and others with the truth. As our minds are renewed by knowing the truth, not only will we find lasting freedom, but also we will be able to discern God's will. How will we be able to do that? We will have a greater understanding of who God is, what His character is like, and will be able to recognize truth. When you know the real thing, you'll never accept a counterfeit.

Lord, You are good. Regardless of my circumstances, regardless of my ever-changing emotions, regardless of what other people tell me – You are GOOD! Help me to renew my mind through the truth of Your word today. Help me to stand with the helmet of salvation snapped snuggly on my head, with the breastplate of righteousness covering my heart, with the belt of truth wrapped around my waist, with the shoes of the gospel of peace guiding my every step, with the shield of faith lifted up to extinguish every flaming arrow of the enemy, and with the sword of the Spirit, which is the word of God, to cut through every lie, false teaching, and accusation of the enemy. Reveal to me the areas of my beliefs about You that have been infiltrated, broken, or worn down by the attacks of the enemy on my life. Your desire is to give me a future and a hope. Your desire is that I would prosper and be in good health. Your desire is that I would be full of joy and surrounded by love. Your desire is to give me the desires of my heart as I delight myself in You. Your desire is that I would taste and see that You are good! Lord, forgive me for believing wrongly about You. Heal my heart. Reveal Your truth. Renew my mind. In Jesus name. Amen!

KRISTIN REEG

6. REAPPLY

Normally, when we think of reapply, our immediate thought is to do something again. However, if our results the first time were not desirable, then we hesitate to repeat that action.

But what if God was asking you to reapply your faith in a certain area? What if He is asking you to reapply your hope? What if He is asking you to trust again despite what it looks like, despite the naysayers, despite what your emotions are screaming?

In the book of Habakkuk, the Lord said, "Write down the revelation and make it plain on tablets so that a herald may run with it. For the revelation awaits an appointed time; it speaks of the end and will not prove false. Though it linger, wait for it; it will certainly come and will not delay" (2:2-3 NIV).

What's your vision? What's your heart's desire? It's time to rewrite the vision. It's time to reapply your faith in written form and avoid vagueness. Make it plain so that anyone (especially the angels of God) who reads it has no doubt of what you are desiring! Reapply. Make a new request or a similar request a second time. God hasn't denied the request; He simply wants you to know and express to Him what it is you truly desire!

7. REFRESH

In the Internet Age, we often think of refresh in relation to our browsers. We refresh the page to see if there are any updates or to try to fix a link that's broken.

Perhaps the meaning is much deeper than that. What if the Lord wants to refresh your soul? What if He wants to invade those areas of sorrow and disappointment and refresh them with His joy? Oh, that we would learn to rest in His love!

The Lord delights over you with singing and dancing! He is constantly inviting you to His praise party! He has turned our mourning into dancing; He has turned our sorrows into joy!

The joy of the Lord is our strength! But it is so much more than that! The Hebrew word for strength can also be translated as protection or power! As He refreshes you with His joy and removes those layers of despair, disappointment, and depression, He enables you to move forward with new strength, divine protection, and His power!

Lord, come refresh our souls today! Let us feel the rain of Your presence. Infuse our hearts with Your joy! Let the sound of laughter be heard from our mouths! May Your praises ever be on our lips! Awaken our hearts to Your good deeds! May Your joy, power, and strength refresh us and protect our hearts from which the wellsprings of life flow! In Jesus name!

8. RECONCILE

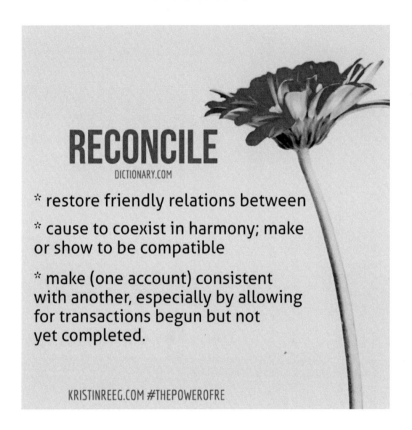

RECONCILE
DICTIONARY.COM

* restore friendly relations between

* cause to coexist in harmony; make or show to be compatible

* make (one account) consistent with another, especially by allowing for transactions begun but not yet completed.

KRISTINREEG.COM #THEPOWEROFRE

God is reconciling accounts in Heaven! The places where the enemy has stolen, he will be forced to repay. The places where you were supposed to gain interest on a payout, and you haven't... get ready! Proverbs 6:30-31 reminds us that if a thief is caught, he must repay seven times – even if it bankrupts him! Who would like to see the devil bankrupted because he has to pay back the saints of God?!? The books are being reconciled in Heaven!

Jesus said, "Still other seed fell on good soil, where it produced a crop—a hundred, sixty or thirty times what was sown," (Matthew 13:8 NIV). You have planted seeds in GOOD soil, and you have not yet seen a return on your investment. Again, I hear the Lord saying, that the books in Heaven are being reconciled! The angels are being deployed to reap the crops in your fields that are ready for harvest! Get ready to receive!

9. REFINE

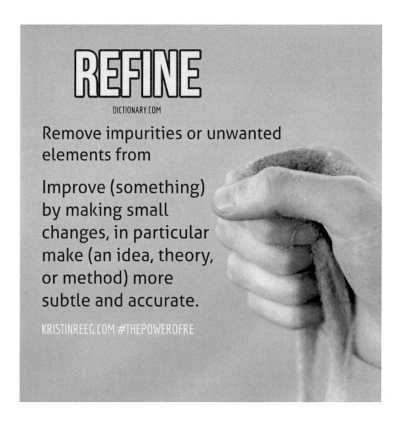

REFINE

DICTIONARY.COM

Remove impurities or unwanted elements from

Improve (something) by making small changes, in particular make (an idea, theory, or method) more subtle and accurate.

KRISTINREEG.COM #THEPOWEROFRE

Our trials are not to meant to destroy us; rather, they are designed to remove impurities or undesired elements from our character. The fire of affliction comes to purify us as silver or gold. With every trial, with every temptation, there is an invitation from our Father to rise up! He is calling His Bride to new levels of holiness.

God has called His people to be set apart. He is returning for a pure and spotless Bride. Refinement is designed to elevate us. Its purpose is to make us a better version of ourselves.

Imagine a kitchen with every cupboard and drawer open. Some are only open a small amount, while others are open all the way. How do you feel? (I can feel some of you cringing at the thought!) Okay, now go through the kitchen and shut all the drawers and cupboards. Now how do you feel? Peace and order have been restored to the kitchen! This is refinement. A small change renewed the peace in the kitchen.

Imagine that your soul (mind, will, and emotions) is a kitchen with everything open. When the Lord comes to refine us, He is illuminating the open doors. He is inviting us to shut them in order to keep the thief from stealing, killing, and destroying our joy, faith, and identity.

Oh Beloved, let us join with the Spirit of God and allow His refinement in our lives! Let us not live a life of regret and open doors, but instead allow the Lord to show us and help us to close the doors within our souls.

10. RETURN

RETURN

WEBSTERSDICTIONARY1828.COM

• To come or go back to the same place.

• To come to the same state; as, to return from bondage to a state of freedom.

• To come again; to revisit.

• To show fresh signs of mercy.

KRISTINREEG.COM #THEPOWEROFRE

Have you ever been driving and veered just a little bit too far to the left or right? Have you driven over the ridges on the highway that alert you to return to your lane? If we're not paying attention, we can drive the highway of life ignoring the warning signs of the ridges in the road. The longer we ignore them, the rougher the ride, and the more damage we do to ourselves (and potentially others.)

The Lord is offering us an invitation today. He wants to help us get back into our lane. He wants to smooth out our rides, and bless us. But in order for that to happen, we have to choose to return to Him.

I can hear some of you saying, "Return? But I haven't left!" We can be physically present, but emotionally detached. We can be spiritually attuned, but our hearts scattered. It doesn't take much when driving at 80 miles an hour to veer out of the lane. If you are one degree off course, and maintain it for a long time, you will find that you are a great distance from your intended destination.

"I will give them a heart to know me, that I am the Lord. They will be my people, and I will be their God, for they will return to me with all their heart," (Jeremiah 24:7 NIV).

Lord, we give You permission to examine our hearts. Reveal to us where our souls have veered to the right or left. Show us where we have gone outside of our lane, and where our hearts have grown cold to You. The greatest commandment is to love You with ALL our heart, soul, mind, and strength. We repent of and renounce the lies that we can find satisfaction for our souls anywhere else other than in Your presence. You are our joy! We choose this day to return to You with all our heart! We receive Your forgiveness and Your mercy. As we return, give us a heart to know You in Jesus name!

11. REVOKE

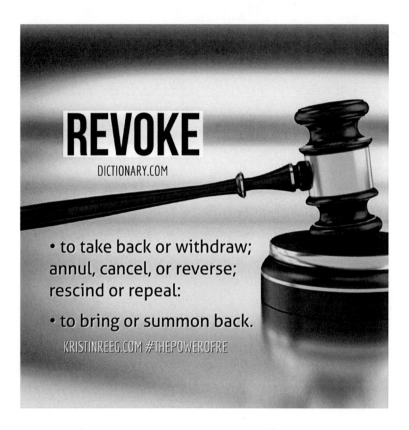

REVOKE
DICTIONARY.COM

• to take back or withdraw; annul, cancel, or reverse; rescind or repeal:

• to bring or summon back.
KRISTINREEG.COM #THEPOWEROFRE

Through the death and resurrection of Jesus Christ, the power of the enemy was revoked. Jesus went to Hell and took the keys to the enemy's own kingdom.

Some of us have given the enemy license to wreak havoc in our lives through our actions, attitudes, and beliefs. It's time to revoke his license and stop him (and his minions) from driving all over our yards.

There is still power in the blood of Jesus! God's mercies are still new every morning. God's grace is still sufficient! But there is action required on our part. If someone came to your house and broke in, would you lay out a welcome mat for him to come again? Would you put all your precious items on display and leave your doors unlocked? Of course not!

And yet, unknowingly, we give the enemy access to our souls through unforgiveness, bitter roots, and ungodly choices.

Oh that we would check our own hearts! Lord, show us the areas within our lives where we need the power of Your blood to forgive us so that the enemy's license in our lives can be revoked! Show us where we have given him free reign, and we will repent. We desire for our relationship with You to be pure, and we no longer want to be frenemy's with the evil one. As we choose to let go, we ask that You would step in as judge and jury and remove every legal right the enemy has to torment us. You are good! You are for us not against us! You desire the best for us! You want us to prosper and be in good health even as our souls prosper! Have mercy on us today, and reveal what needs to heal within us in Jesus name.

12. RELEASE

We desire freedom, and yet we choose prison. For many of us, we willingly walk into the proverbial cell and shut the door even when we hold the key to unlock it in our very hands.

I'll never forget the day the Lord whispered to me that the same blood that washed me of my sin is the same blood that washed others of the sin that they have done to me.

It's time to unlock the door and step out of our self-inflicted prisons. It's time to release others and ourselves from the judgments, debts, and demand for apologies. My friends, it's time to forgive. Yes, I don't know what you did. You're right. I don't know what was done to you. But regardless of who did what to whom, we will never move forward if we choose to remain in a prison cell erected by our own emotions.

Each day we are given a choice: we can receive or reject the new mercies that God provides. If we choose to receive them, then we also need to extend them to others. If we choose to reject them, then we have denied the cross of Christ and made ourselves judge and jury which only leads to condemnation. We will never be able to repay the debt of our own mistakes, wrong-doings, and willful choices. Therefore, the wise choice is to accept God's mercy and release it to others as well.

Forgiveness is not a one time event. We do not simply open our mouths, let the words flow off our tongues, and call it done. There is an adversary that desires to devour you. His full-time occupation is to remind you of everything anyone has ever done to hurt you. He stands as the accuser of the brethren, and he wants you to pick up the offense that you already forgave. Forgiveness is a choice that must be chosen repeatedly every time the incident comes into our minds. As we continue to forgive and release ourselves and/or others from whatever we believe we are owed, our emotions will align with our choice. But if we do not continually choose forgiveness, then the emotions of anger, bitterness, hatred, etc will fester and contaminate our hearts.

Choose freedom today. Choose to release the captives. Choose to release the prisoners. Choose to unlock the shackles on your heart and receive the mercy of God! And once you have received it, you have it to give away. We cannot give what we do not possess.

KRISTIN REEG

13. RECOVER

RECOVER

DICTIONARY.COM

- Return to a normal state of health, mind, or strength.
- Find or regain possession of (something stolen or lost).
- Regain or secure (compensation) by means of a legal process or subsequent profits.

KRISTINREEG.COM #THEPOWEROFRE

What has the enemy stolen from you? What has caused you great sorrow? In 1 Samuel 30, David and his mighty men returned to Ziklag to find the city burnt to the ground and their wives and children taken captive by an enemy army. The Bible says that David and his men wept aloud until they had no strength left to weep (vs. 4).

Oh, how life can sometimes steal our breath away! There are days when the trials of life consume our souls to the degree that we weep until we have no strength, no tears left to cry. (Or maybe that's just me!)

In 1 Samuel 30, David inquired of the Lord. In short, God advises David to pursue, overtake, and recover all (vs. 8). Ten verses later, "David recovered everything the Amalekites had taken, including his two wives" (vs. 18).

There is hope of recovery! While David would need to rebuild Ziklag, he was able to recover what the enemy stolen, and he gained more! Friends, it's time to rise up and pursue the enemy! Pursue! Overtake! Recover all! Don't stand idly by and watch the enemy steal your relationships or your stuff! It's time to engage the enemy! But let us battle wisely! David inquired of the Lord before he went after the thief. God knows all. The time of RECOVERY is now! Seek Him for the strategy to enable you to overtake and recover all!

14. REDEFINE

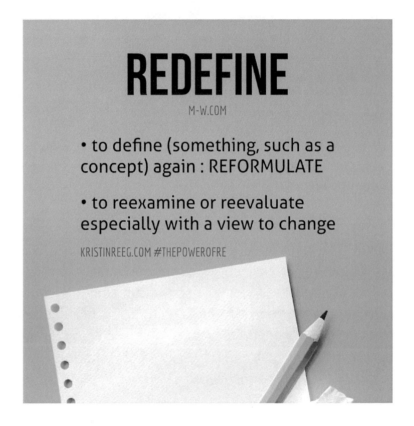

WORDS ARE POWERFUL. They have the ability to build up and tear down. They can create life or breed death. It is not just the utterance of a word that brings forth its power; it is our belief or faith associated with it that empowers its reality.

Jesus asked His disciples two questions in Matthew 16. First, who do the people say that I am? Secondly, who do you say that I am?

These are questions that we, too, must ask; however, we need to ask them about ourselves. We need to take some time and evaluate ourselves. 1) Who do others say you are? How would others label you? 2) Who do you say that you are? What labels do you put on yourself? And let's add one more, 3) Who does God say you are? How would He label you? Look at the answers. How do they compare? What is true? What is false? What is true, but you'd like to change it?

Every day we have an opportunity to confirm or deny the labels that we wear as well as the labels that have been put on us. It's time to redefine who we are and allow our hearts to believe that we can truly live up to who God says we are. The redefining process takes time; it's not a onetime event. As we surrender to the Spirit of God, our mind, will, and emotions are continually being transformed to mirror like the image of Jesus on earth.

Lord, awaken our hearts to receive how You define us! Give us the courage to re-examine and reevaluate our words, thoughts, actions, and labels.

15. RECEIVE

RECEIVE

WEBSTERSDICTIONARY1828.COM

1. To take, as a thing offered or sent; to accept.

2 . To take as due or as a reward.

3. To take or obtain from another in any manner, and either good or evil.

4. To take, as a thing communicated;

5. To take or obtain intellectually;

6. To embrace

7. To allow; to hold; to retain;

KRISTINREEG.COM #THEPOWEROFRE

There is a common thread in most of the definitions of the word receive. The first five definitions start with "to take". The number five often represents grace. Consider this: grace is needed to empower us to receive.

In order to fully receive something, we need to be willing to take what is offered. There is a grand difference between a gift and a loan. Gifts are given freely with no expectation of payback. Loans are contracts with terms for payback explicitly stated.

"For it is by grace you have been saved, through faith — and this is not from yourselves, it is the gift of God— not by works, so that no one can boast," (Ephesians 2:8-9 NIV).

God freely offers us the gift of salvation which is the deliverance from the wages of sin and death. God loves each one of us so much that He provided each of us with a measure of faith; therefore, we are able to receive His grace to take His gift.

God gives us the gift of salvation through the death and resurrection of Jesus Christ. It is a gift, not a loan. God does not expect us to pay Him back for forgiving our sins and securing our eternal destiny. He simply asks that we take what He is freely offering. Gifts are God's love language! Let's open our hearts to receive today!

16. RECTIFY

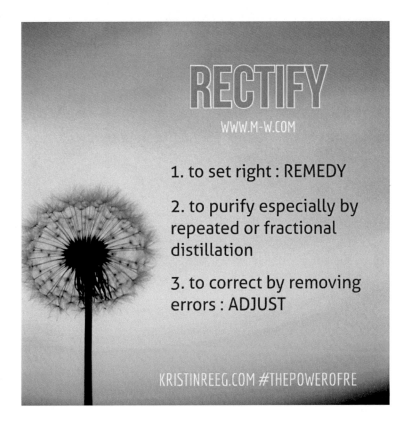

I cannot begin to comprehend how difficult the battles have been for you recently. I do not know the tears you've cried, the prayers you've prayed, or the weariness you've experienced, but this I DO know: God is not only fighting with you; He is fighting for you.

I heard the Lord whisper that He is rectifying things for His people. He is going to make things right. He is entering the timeline of our lives and correcting the crooked places and making them straight. Those areas where the enemy thought he won... NOPE. GOD has the last word, and I prophesy to you right now that God is about to manifest Himself in your life as your Defender. He is arising with a sword in His hand. God is going to rectify your situation. When the enemy spread his lies about you, God's going to rectify it. When the enemy falsely accused you and heaped shame upon you, God's going to rectify it. When the enemy stole your opportunities, God's going to rectify it.

"You won't have to fight this battle yourselves; the Eternal your God, who always goes ahead of you, will fight for you just as He did in Egypt—you saw Him do it," (Deuteronomy 1:30 VOICE)!

Allow my pastor's heart to give you a word of balance along with this awesome encouragement. Seek the Lord; ask Him what situation or situations in your life to which this applies. Too many times we assume that the word is for one thing when that is not what God said. Don't receive with presumption. Receive the word. Seek the Lord. Then allow Him to decide the method that He will use to bring about a desired and beneficial outcome for you. XOXO

17. REVEAL

Adam and Eve played Hide and Seek with God, but that is not the game He desires to play. God wants to play Seek and Seek with us. "You will seek me and find me when you seek me with all your heart," (Jeremiah 29:13 NIV).

The Creator of the universe, the maker of heaven and earth longs to be known by us. Before we could ever pronounce the name Jesus, He was already calling out to us. He knows our names. He knows when we sit and when we rise. He knows every thought we have, and yet He does not condemn us for them. Instead, He longs to illuminate His love to such a degree that we no longer have them.

To Moses, God revealed Himself as the I AM THAT I AM. In other words, what you need Him to be. He will be. Do you need a friend? Do you need a Father? Do you need a Counselor? Do you need someone to be with you? Do you need someone to defend you? Do you need someone to fight for you? Do you need a savior? Do you need a deliverer? Do you need comforted? Do you need to feel loved? Do you need provision? Do you just need to know someone sees you?

Oh Lord, You are good! You are the great I AM!!! Would You reveal Yourself to us today? Would You come and show us in tangible ways that You are the One our hearts long for? Would You display Your character? Would You show us the truth about who You are to break through the lies that we have believed about You? Forgive us for believing that You caused our suffering! Forgive us for blaming You for the things that have happened in our lives! Forgive us for not seeking to know who You are! Forgive us for believing what everyone else has told us about You! Come and be our healer today! Mend our broken hearts and reveal to us who we, as individuals, need You to be in our lives. We choose to believe again that we will taste and see that You are good! In Jesus name. Amen.

KRISTIN REEG

18. REMEDY

REMEDY

WEBSTERSDICTIONARY1828.COM

1. To cure; to heal;
2. To cure; to remove, as an evil;
3. To repair; to remove mischief;

KRISTINREEG.COM #THEPOWEROFRE

The battles have been so intense these past couple of years. Many were not sure they would make it through; some were not sure if they wanted to make it through. We know that the enemy doesn't play fair. And while our spirits and our minds know that our battles are not against flesh and blood, the enemy of our souls has wreaked havoc as the Accuser of the Brethren. While his attacks certainly feel personal, it's really not about us.

It's about discrediting God who lives within us. The enemy longs for us to deny our faith, to curse God, and to step away from the most perfect remedy that man was ever given: the blood of Jesus Christ.

We overcome the Accuser of the Brethren by the blood of the Lamb (Jesus Christ, God's own son) and the word of our testimony. (Revelation 12:11)

Do not be deceived. God sees you. He is not ignorant of the tears you have cried, the wounds you have endured, or the battles you have withstood. He is not standing idly by withholding His protection, provision, or presence. I cannot begin to fathom the trauma that some of my brothers and sisters in Christ have experienced. I do not claim to have all the answers as to why bad things happen to good people. I do not know why God allows the enemy to war so intensely against us. But this one thing I do know: His name is Emmanuel, God with us. He promised to never leave us or forsake us. And God IS a promise keeper!

Jesus is the remedy for the evil we have experienced. He is the remedy for our broken hearts and our wrongdoings. He is Jehovah Rapha, the God who heals. May our hearts receive the cure for the pain these past couple of years have caused to our souls. God IS going to turn your mourning into dancing. He IS going to give you beauty for ashes. He IS going to remove the spirit of heaviness from your presence and give you a garment of praise! Expect the oil of joy to once again flow through you!

KRISTIN REEG

19. RESOLUTE

The Apostle Paul said that in Christ we live and move and have our being (Acts 17:38). This means as Christians we are living in two realities simultaneously: we live in a natural world ruled by our five senses; we also are part of a spiritual world that greatly influences our natural world. The ruler of the spiritual realm is Jesus Christ, the King of kings. He is the Word made flesh. He is the living Bible. And so we choose moment by moment, knowingly and unknowingly, which world we allow to rule and reign.

People of faith are not superheroes. They are not endowed with superpowers. They are resolute. They have become admirably and unwaveringly set in their belief of the reality and the truth of Jesus Christ. They have chosen to allow His word and His promises to become their reality – even more than what their very own eyes see! This is how they can say that they walk by faith and not sight. They are undaunted by circumstances, knowing that God will work in them and through them to bring about an unforetold blessing.

It is not that these Christians are out of touch with reality; their reality is simply in another realm. The prophet Isaiah said this, "Because the Lord, the Eternal, helps me I will not be disgraced; so, I set my face like a rock, confident that I will not be ashamed," (Isaiah 50:7 VOICE). They are utterly convinced and determined to see God's will, God's goodness, and God's purpose fulfilled in their lives.

This, my friends, is the faith that moves mountains. You don't need a ton of it. In fact, Jesus said you only need enough to fill a mustard seed. Do you have a sliver of resolute hope within you that refuses to doubt? Grab ahold of that mustard seed of faith, and present it to God for your situation. Confess the doubt. Confess the fear. Don't pretend it's not there. Bring it into the light, and allow God to speak His truth to your heart. As you focus on His goodness, you will find that the things of earth, the trials and the tribulations, will grow strangely dim in comparison to His glory and grace.

God is for you not against you. He's not angry with our questions or our fears. He simply wants us to admit we have them, then He can release His love to expel them and increase our faith so that we see those mountains move!

KRISTIN REEG

20. REVIVE

REVIVE
DICTIONARY.COM

- restore to life or consciousness.
- regain life, consciousness, or strength.
- give new strength or energy to.

KRISTINREEG.COM #THEPOWEROFRE

Revive means essentially to live again. What if the revival God is seeking is for us to learn to actually live? What if He desires for our hearts to beat with His? What if He desires to heal our souls so that we no longer walk around numb? What if God's concept of revival is to restore joy to our weary souls? What if His concept is to bring freedom to such a degree that we actually feel like living? What if God's idea of an abundant life was more about relationships and less about things?

My friends, the more we focus on things or stuff, the harder our hearts become. When our hearts become hard, we can easily feel dead inside. We are created for relationship. We are designed for community. The abundant life comes with authenticity and vulnerability with those we can trust with our hearts. And, truth be told, it comes with a life of repentance. Repentance cleanses the soul. It removes the weeds that have contaminated the garden of our hearts. As the weeds are removed, the roots have room to grow. We find that we can breathe again knowing that Jesus Christ has already paid the price; we are forgiven.

Repentance isn't a scary thing. Too often we over-spiritualize it, or we think it only pertains to the really "bad" stuff we do. Sometimes we allow certain emotions, which we were never intended to befriend, to become our long-time companions.

True confession: I had to repent of holding onto sorrow. I had allowed disappointment, discouragement, and despair to weigh down my soul like a warm blanket on a winter morning. That's right. I welcomed sorrow. I expected it. But that life is contrary to what God promises. When I chose to repent from holding onto sorrow like Linus's blanket, my soul came alive again. I was revived! Joy returned. I could laugh again, and the kind of laugh that refilled my cup instead of masking my pain.

While this may seem odd, repentance is addictive in the most amazing way. We don't need to go on a witch hunt in our lives to find things for which we should repent. The Psalmist asked God to search him and let him know the areas in his heart and mind that needed cleansed (Ps. 139). David asked God to create in him a clean heart and to restore the joy of his salvation (Ps. 51). Let God do the searching, then agreed with Him. This will cleanse our souls, restore our joy, and purify us! When we are revived with clean hands and pure hearts, we will see God move in miraculous ways in us and through us.

KRISTIN REEG

21. REAL

I've been thinking a lot about "The Velveteen Rabbit" by Margery Williams. The stuffed rabbit was on a journey to become real. When it was first given to the child, it was perfect. But as the child began to love it, the fur wore off; there were rips and tears that had been stitched; it may have even lost an eye. Nevertheless, it was in the loving and being loved that the rabbit become real.

Oh, that we would learn that it is not in our perfection, but it is in our brokenness that we become real. It is in allowing ourselves to be loved and to love that we find our greatest joys! Unfortunately, we live in a fallen world. And where there is falling, there are breaks and bruises. Some breaks leave scars. Some bruises still get bumped. And sometimes, in an effort to protect our breaks and our bruises, we strive to stuff it all inside. We strive to project an outer image that hides the true beauty of our authenticity.

We long to be seen and known, and yet our fears of being seen and known for who we truly are are just as intense as watching a suspenseful movie. Even when we know what is about to come next, we still react with a scream, a jump, or a gasp. We fear being real because we fear the pain that comes with it.

But what if we pressed past the pain? What if we faced the fear? What if we allowed ourselves to be seen, known, and loved? What if our fears were nothing more than smoke and mirrors? What if they were illusions that were designed to keep us from experiencing real, genuine, true love? What if this is the fear that builds walls instead of bridges in our relationships?

God loves you. It's not a trite saying. His love is true. His love is real. Many are afraid of His love because we have this image of sinners in the hands of an angry God ready to pummel us for our wrongs. This is not the real God. In fact, Jesus Christ chose to die for us out of His love for us before we were ever able to whisper His name. What if God was trying to show His love to you through your relationships? Think about the people in your life that restore your soul, those who with a word or a hug can fill your heart and give you strength to press on. These are the people that most often can be trusted, and to whom we can show our real selves.

The more willing we become to remove the "stuffing", the more real we will become. As we learn to love and be loved, we will find our capacity for love has grown. And with love comes faith and hope, and a whole new perspective on God, on love, and even brokenness.

KRISTIN REEG

22. RESILIENT

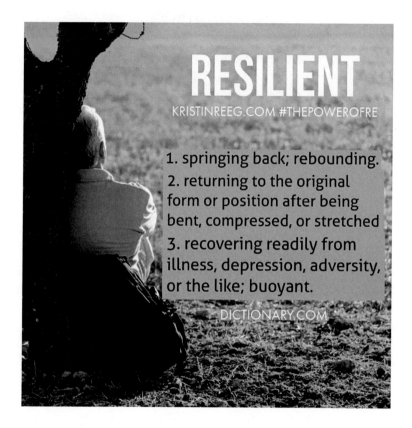

It's not about if trials, tribulations, or persecution will come; it's about our reaction when they come. Every moment of every day we have a choice. We can accept the thoughts that run through our minds regardless of the emotions attached, or we can filter them through the light of the Word of God.

We don't have to receive every thought we think. We don't have to believe everything we hear. Uncomfortable circumstances are part of living in a sin ridden world, but how we choose to respond will determine the residual and lasting effects.

Have you ever watched a tree in a storm? If it's root system is strong, the wind could toss it like a rubber pencil, and yet it would remain standing. When the storm ceases, the tree returns to its original position. It is resilient.

Father God, would You give us the discernment to know which thoughts are safe to keep? Would You help us throw out and discard the ones that come to accuse us, our loved ones, and/or our coworkers?

Holy Spirit, You are the revealer of truth. We give You permission to open our eyes, open our hearts, and open our ears to see, hear, and receive the truth. Psalm one says that You desire for us to be like a tree planted by water. Oh, that we would flourish even in dry seasons! Oh that we would remain confident and steadfast even as the storms of life try to uproot us and deny Your name. Help us to forgive those who have hurt us, those who have deceived or abused us, and those who have betrayed us. May we be like Paul, forgetting those things which are behind and pressing on toward what is ahead to win the prize for which God has called us heavenward in Christ Jesus. In Jesus name, amen.

23. REJOICE

REJOICE

KRISTINREEG.COM #THEPOWEROFRE

• To experience joy and gladness in a high degree

• To make joyful; to gladden

WEBSTERSDICTIONARY1828.COM

Rejoice! We all love to have joy and be glad in heart! But some days it is harder than others to achieve. We've heard it said, "It's a choice to rejoice!" Notice that this is most often said from an extremely happy person to someone who isn't.

Truth be told, I've wanted to hang up the phone or throw something at the person who says it to me when I'm just not "there". Joy is not a light switch. We don't just turn it on or off on command. Joy is like a geyser that bubbles up within our soul and explodes outward. We can't force it, but we can ignite it.

Joy is a powerful weapon that is often misunderstood. Laughter shifts atmospheres, releases happy chemicals in our brains, and restores our souls.

When I struggle with joy, I do a couple of things to stir it up again.

1. I check my thoughts. Is what I'm thinking about full of faith, hope, and love, or am I auditioning to be the next Debbie Downer?

2. I choose to bring to remembrance things that make me laugh. I had a roommate that once unknowingly touched a bird. She freaked out so much that she ran smack into the glass door, finally opened it, and proceeded to do laps around the coffee table screaming! It still cracks me up!

3. I think about the people in my life that bring joy to my heart. I think about something they said, they did, or they gave me. These thoughts remind me that I'm loved and cared about.

4. I intentionally search for things on various social media platforms that will make me laugh (keep it clean!).

5. I drink more coffee. (This is probably the first thing I do in all sincerity! Ha!) It's true; there is a comfort found in hot liquids that simply brings a smile to my face.

These are just some of the things I do to actively participate in restoring joy to my life. There are a billion other ways, and your personality will determine what works for you. I know you may be shocked that I didn't list the things I need to be grateful for as my first thing, or that my answers weren't exceptionally "spiritual". Gratefulness is awesome, and it DOES bring joy. But sometimes we need non-spiritual solutions. And isn't it nice to know that it's okay to be human?

KRISTIN REEG

24. RENAME

When think about naming, our first thought is normally people or pets. I feel a charge in my spirit to rename our seasons, rename our days. As I'm writing this, it's a Monday. Our society has attached a lot of negative emotions or connotations to Mondays. Rename it! When we change the name of something, we shift the way we look at it, the way we approach it, and even in some ways the way we attack it.

We have an adversary, an enemy, who works 24/7 to steal, kill, and destroy the works of God in the earth. As society begins to elevate the things of darkness with witches, warlocks, and the devil, I want to remind us all that the devil is not our friend. He is the enemy! Rename him as your enemy! He is not for you; in fact, he hates you with so much passion that he sends special forces of demons to hinder your progress in every area. He whispers lies to you about you and about others. His sole purpose is to bring you to a point of utter destruction that you deny and curse God.

People are not your enemy; the spirits operating behind them are the enemy. Forgive people, and use your anger and frustration in prayer against your real foe. As darkness strives to cloud your day, be the light. Be strong in the Lord, and recognize that your enemy is not flesh and blood. Put on the full armor of God, and keep on praying for all the saints! **YOU ARE AN OVERCOMER!** And Revelation tells us that those who overcome receive a new name!

(Ephesians 6, Revelation 2)

25. RELIABLE

Our God is reliable. He is dependable. He has been tested and tried throughout all of time, and His promises remain the same: He will never leave us. He will never forsake us. He will not fail us (Joshua 1).

Oh, we may have moments when we feel that God forgot about us. We may have moments when we feel as though He failed us. It is in these very moments that need to remember His character. He is reliable. He will never let us down. Does this mean that everything in our lives will work out according to our expectations? Hardly! But regardless of what our circumstances may dictate, we can trust in His unfailing love for us. We can trust in His goodness.

The Apostle Paul was shipwrecked, beaten, and blinded, and yet, it was he who confessed that he knew that all things work together for good for those who love God and are called according to His purposes. Not everything that happens to us is good, but God is trustworthy. He will maneuver and shift either our perspectives or our situations to bring about goodness and reveal His glory.

Oh Lord, You alone know our hearts. You know the fears we fight, the doubts we deny, and burdens we bury. Would You rise up among us? Would You show Yourself to be our defender, avenger, and provider? Manifest Your trustworthiness and reliability in our lives. Give us a sign of Your goodness that our enemies may see it and be put to shame. We confess with our mouths and to choose to believe in our hearts that You love us and fight for us. Do for us, God, what we cannot do for ourselves in Jesus name.

26. REGAL

REGAL

KRISTINREEG.COM #THEPOWEROFRE

1: of, relating to, or suitable for a king

2: of notable excellence or magnificence : SPLENDID

WWW.M-W.COM

Jesus is King! He has conquered sin, death, and the grave. There is nothing in our lives that He is incapable of handling or overcoming. He is the ruler over all.

As I was listening to the song *"Worthy of It All"* by David Brymer, I heard the Lord ask me, *"Do you really believe that I'm worthy of it all?"*

Me: Yes, Lord. I do believe.

"Do you believe that I'm worthy of your fear?"

Me: Wait. What?!? But isn't fear a bad thing? Does God really want my fear?

"All means ALL. Can you give it to Me? Can you give Me your fear?"

In all transparency, I wept – like ugly cry wept. Jesus is King of my good, and He is King of my bad. He empowers me in the things of God, and He longs for me to receive His love and forgiveness in the areas in which I struggle.

Oh Beloved! How He longs for you and I to fully receive His love! How He longs to truly be found worthy of it all! Everything – the good, the bad, the ugly – places we willingly bring to the light as well as places we strive to keep hidden. He longs for us to understand His majesty not because He is a harsh ruler! Not at all! He is full of love and compassion. His desire is mercy, not punishment. Beloved, I encourage you to go before the King of kings today and offer as a sacrifice your fear, doubt, insecurity, uncertainty, etc. Watch what beauty the King will create from the ashes of our hidden things.

27. REVISIT

Do you have a word from the Lord that you have placed upon the shelf of "someday"? Do you have a heart's desire that has remained unfulfilled? Are there things that you want to do with God that in your mind still seem impossible?

The Psalmist declared, "Make God the utmost delight

and pleasure of your life, and he will provide for you what you desire the most. Give God the right to direct your life, and as you trust him along the way you'll find he pulled it off perfectly! He will appear as your righteousness, as sure as the dawning of a new day. He will manifest as your justice, as sure and strong as the noonday sun. Quiet your heart in his presence and pray; keep hope alive as you long for God to come through for you. And don't think for a moment that the wicked in their prosperity are better off than you," (Psalm 37:4-7 TPT).

Oh Beloved, I hear the whisper of the Spirit of God. It's time to dust off those dreams. It's time to put those desires back in a place of prominence, a place where they can be seen for hope and faith to arise. God is not slow in keeping His promises. Every promise is fulfilled in His divine timing. And while the promises and the desires are FOR us, there fulfillment is for the glory of God.

Revisit the areas that once brought disappointment. Bring them again to the Father with a heart overflowing with love and gratitude for who He is and what the Son has done. As our greatest desire becomes to know Him more, He'll bring glory to His name through the display of His goodness in our lives. May His goodness through us become a lighthouse for others to know Him too.

It's okay. There's no need to fear disappointment again.

I hear the Lord saying, *"It's safe to trust Me. What is your heart's desire? Make it known to Me. Seek Me to know Me. I will be found by you, and our joy will be complete. Open your heart to once again receive My love and know My voice. You will find that I am not far and distant, but I am as close as a whisper. It's okay. It's safe to trust Me."*

KRISTIN REEG

28. REVOLUTION

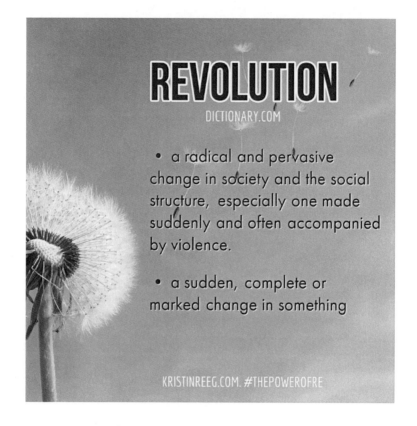

We cry out for revival, but there can be no revival without a personal revolution. Revolution speaks of change, radical change. It speaks of an overthrow of a governmental body. Too many in our society are pushing for a national, political revolution when what we really need is a change of government in our own hearts.

"Who may ascend the mountain of the Lord? Who may stand in his holy place? The one who has clean hands and a pure heart, who does not trust in an idol or swear by a false god. They will receive blessing from the Lord and vindication from God their Savior," (Psalm 24:3-5 NIV).

Oh Lord, forgive us! Forgive us individually and forgive us corporately! We are a people of unclean lips! We are a people of unclean hands! We have filled our hearts with darkness and worldly pleasures even while claiming to seek Your face! We wear our badge of Christiandom, and yet our hearts are far from You! We give you lip service while selling our souls to the nearest idol! Forgive us, God! You said that if Your people who are called by Your name would humble themselves and pray and turn from our wicked ways that You would hear from heaven! You promised that You would forgive our sin and heal our land! Start with the soil in our souls! Start with us! Plow up the fallow ground and water our souls with the cleansing power of Your blood. Wash away our iniquities and let Your forgiveness and love overtake us! It is Your kindness that leads us to repentance.

Lord, I ask for an angel of revolution to be sent to every person who reads this and comes into agreement. By the power of unity, manifest a change so radical in our spirits and souls that it births the coming reformation.

Ignite a fresh revival that we understand what it means to live again! We ask for Your assistance to destroy our idols. Wipe their names from our lips, and may the name of the One True God be the only one we proclaim! Help us to prepare the way for the King of Glory! "Who is this King of glory? The Lord strong and mighty, the Lord mighty in battle," (Psalm 24:8 NIV). Come, Lord! Make Your presence known in our midst! For You are good, and Your love endures forever! In Jesus name. Amen.

KRISTIN REEG

29. REFORM

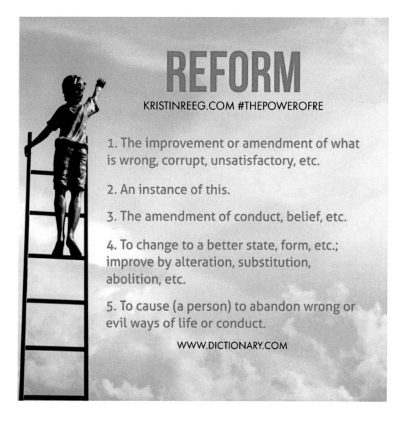

We speak of the days of old. We speak of the courage of Martin Luther to hang his 95 Theses on the door of the church. We speak of the Reformation, but do we actually understand what reform means?

The word reformation actually means "the act of reforming; the state of being reformed." Therefore, in order to understand the past reformation and to look ahead with anticipation for the coming reformation, we must understand what it means to reform.

Reform means to improve, to change for the better, and to abandon wrong ways of life. As my dear friend, Jeana, highlighted to me: "It is the act of being re-formed."

The Psalmist reminds us that God knitted us together; He formed us in our mother's womb. At that time, He spoke passion and purpose into our souls. I can imagine God whispering about the good works that He was already preparing for us when we entered into the world. Oh the joy of the angels when we officially arrived on the scene. God had a plan for us perfectly designed before we were ever conceived.

But life happens. We experience pain and trauma. We start to believe lies as though they are truth. These lies begin to mold us and shape us into an image that is opposite of whom we were created to be. Our pure hearts grow dark through the trials and tribulations of life. Our affections have turned to those whom we have carved into our own image, or the image of what we desire. And one day, unbeknownst to us, we are no longer mold-able or pliable. We have become like stone. God, in His unfathomable mercy, seeks to restore us to the image He had of us as He formed us in our mother's womb. He desires to improve our character, change us from glory to glory, and help us abandon our wrong and harmful ways of life.

The Lord said through the prophet Ezekiel, "I will sprinkle clean water on you, and you will be clean; I will cleanse you from all your impurities and from all your idols. I will give you a new heart and put a new spirit in you; I will remove from you your heart of stone and give you a heart of flesh. And I will put my Spirit in you and move you to follow my decrees and be careful to keep my laws," (Ezekiel 36:25-27 NIV).

Lord, would You come with Your love and reform our hearts? We are a people full of pride with hearts hardened by betrayal. Forgive us for seeking a solution to our pain outside of the cross of Christ. Forgive us for prostituting our affections to the lowest bidder. Forgive us for the way that we have come to view ourselves – unworthy of love, unworthy of forgiveness, unworthy of Your grace. We cry out for hope in a hopeless world. We cry out for truth yet cling to the lies that protect our souls, not understanding that it is those very beliefs that hold us captive. But You said that You came to set the prisoner and the captive free. You said that You desire to give us a garment of praise for the spirit of heaviness. You want to give us beauty in exchange for ashes. Awaken our hearts to Your plans and purposes for us! We give You permission to come as the Potter and reform this clay. We want to be pliable in Your hands. Forgive our sins, and mold us into our original design.

Reform us to such a degree that we become a catalyst for the next reformation in the church and in society. Fill our hearts with Your love until every wound is healed in Jesus name.

30. REDEEM

REDEEM

* to buy back : REPURCHASE

* to free from what distresses or harms: such as [captivity, debt, sin]

* to change for the better : REFORM

* repair: restore

* to atone for : EXPIATE

MERRIAM-WEBSTER.COM

In Christian circles, we use the word redeem often. I'm not sure that we are aware of the depth it truly holds. We proclaim that Jesus has redeemed us from the curse of sin and death. Looking at the dictionary definition gives us a much broader and clearer understanding of what that means.

Through the blood sacrifice of Jesus Christ on the cross coupled with His resurrection three days later, we have been redeemed. We are now free from our captivity (that which caused us harm, distress, and debt). Jesus has purchased our sin and shame to make us pure, holy, without spot or blemish. Because of His sacrifice, our lives can be repaired, restored, and reformed.

Oh that we would learn the power in the blood of Jesus! The old hymn still rings true: "There is power, power, wonder-working power in the blood of the Lamb!"

Each of us has areas in our lives that we need God to redeem. What's on your list? Time? Debt? Health? Relationships? Whatever we need can be redeemed! But there's a secret to accessing the power of God. I'm going to tell you, but please keep it yourself. Are you ready? It begins with a relationship with Jesus. Allowing His sacrifice to first wash over our sin and shame so that we can come boldly before the throne of God as clean vessels. Despite what others may claim, redemption and relationship go hand in hand.

God loves us! And He cares about every single detail in our lives. He cries over the injustice. His heart aches over the abuse and rejection. He is not deaf to our petitions and prayers. However, His heart is for us to come to the table like His disciples did. To partake in the bread and the cup renewing our eternal covenant with Him. Redemption comes through the covenant where everything we are is available and accessible to Him. But wait there's more! This covenant is not one sided! It also means that everything He has is available and accessible to us!

Oh Beloved! God wants to first redeem our relationship with Him! As we learn to commune with Him, He will heal our hearts, vindicate us from our accusers, and reveal His restoration in our lives!

He stands at the door and knocks. He wants to come in and eat with us. He desires for us to break bread with Him recognizing that His body was broken to make us whole. He longs to share the cup with us as a symbol of His bloodshed for the forgiveness of our sin and payment for our shame. He urged His disciples to do it upon every remembrance of Him. Let's begin to see the ritual of communion as a meal with Jesus where we exchange our shortcomings for His love and acceptance.

KRISTIN REEG

WORKS CITED

"real." *Webstersdictionary1828.com*. American Dictionary of the English language, 1828. Web. 5 December 2018.

"reapply." *Merriam-Webster.com*. Merriam-Webster, 2011.Web. 8 May 2011.

"receive." *Webstersdictionary1828.com*. American Dictionary of the English language, 1828. Web. 5 December 2018.

"recompense." *Dictionary.com*. Dictionary, 2018. Web. 5 December 2018.

"reconcile." *Dictionary.com*. Dictionary, 2018. Web. 5 December 2018.

"recover." *Dictionary.com*. Dictionary, 2018. Web. 5 December 2018.

"rectify." *Merriam-Webster.com*. Merriam-Webster, 2011.Web. 8 May 2011.

"redeem." *Merriam-Webster.com*. Merriam-Webster, 2011.Web. 8 May 2011.

"redefine." *Merriam-Webster.com*. Merriam-Webster, 2011.Web. 8 May 2011.

"refine." *Dictionary.com*. Dictionary, 2018. Web. 5 December 2018.

"reform." *Dictionary.com.* Dictionary, 2018. Web. 5 December 2018.

"refresh." *Webstersdictionary1828.com.* American Dictionary of the English language, 1828. Web. 5 December 2018.

"regal." *Merriam-Webster.com.* Merriam-Webster, 2011.Web. 8 May 2011.

"rejoice." *Webstersdictionary1828.com.* American Dictionary of the English language, 1828. Web. 5 December 2018.

"rejuvenate." *Merriam-Webster.com.* Merriam-Webster, 2011.Web. 8 May 2011.

"release." *Webstersdictionary1828.com.* American Dictionary of the English language, 1828. Web. 5 December 2018.

"reliable." *Merriam-Webster.com.* Merriam-Webster, 2011.Web. 8 May 2011.

"remedy." *Webstersdictionary1828.com.* American Dictionary of the English language, 1828. Web. 5 December 2018.

"rename." *Merriam-Webster.com.* Merriam-Webster, 2011.Web. 8 May 2011.

"renew." *Dictionary.com.* Dictionary, 2018. Web. 5 December 2018.

"resilient." *Dictionary.com.* Dictionary, 2018. Web. 5 December 2018.

"resolute." *Dictionary.com*. Dictionary, 2018.
Web. 5 December 2018.

"restore." *Dictionary.com*. Dictionary, 2018.
Web. 5 December 2018.

"return." *Webstersdictionary1828.com*. American
Dictionary of the English language, 1828. Web. 5
December 2018.

"reveal." *Dictionary.com*. Dictionary, 2018.
Web. 5 December 2018.

"reunion." *Webstersdictionary1828.com*. American
Dictionary of the English language, 1828. Web. 5
December 2018.

"revisit." *Dictionary.com*. Dictionary, 2018.
Web. 5 December 2018.

"revive." *Dictionary.com*. Dictionary, 2018.
Web. 5 December 2018.

"revoke." *Dictionary.com*. Dictionary, 2018.
Web. 5 December 2018.

"revolution." *Dictionary.com*. Dictionary, 2018.
Web. 5 December 2018.

KRISTIN REEG

ABOUT THE AUTHOR

Kristin Reeg is an author, inspirational speaker, and encourager with a "Keep It Real" sense of humor. She desires for people to encounter Jesus, to receive His forgiveness, and experience His love. Kristin has earned an MDiv and also an M.A. in Journalism from Regent University, Virginia Beach, VA. In addition, she has obtained a B.A. in Communication from Malone University, Canton, OH. Kristin has authored three books, *Pressing On: Hope for the Weary*, *Sitting in God's Waiting Room*, and *Pressing On: Day by Day*; she is also a frequent writer of Adult Sunday School material for Union Gospel Press.

Leading her first Bible Study at 16, Kristin has more than 25 years of ministry experience. Combining humor, authenticity, and truth, Kristin has a burning passion to inspire, equip, and motivate Christians to live a life of freedom and faith. Her ministry focuses on revealing truth, removing hindrances, and empowering Believers to move forward into their God-given destinies. Armed with God's Word and a cup of coffee, Kristin makes you laugh, gives you permission to cry, and awakens hope within you.

If you would like to invite Kristin to speak at your next event, visit www.kristinreeg.com.

KRISTIN REEG

OTHER BOOKS BY KRISTIN REEG

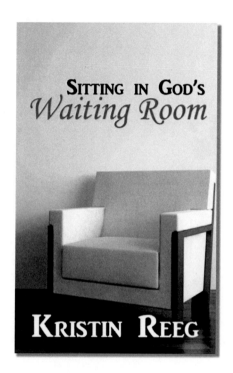

Sitting in God's "waiting room" isn't usually the most comfortable place in the world to be. It has its ups, and it has its downs. Some days, we are full of faith and patience just knowing that God is still in control and that His timing is perfect. Other days, the waiting seems extremely long, and we wonder if the joy of the answer will outweigh the pain of our wait to obtain it. I'm sure we've all had a day or two when we've wondered what we can do to get out of this room and how we can speed up our exit. Nevertheless, we choose to press on driven by something inside our hearts that urges us to keep the faith when everything around us tells us to give up on God and get out of this waiting room.

One thing I do: I press on with Jesus Christ day by day.

It is important to note that Pressing On Day by Day is not your every day devotional. It's different in that the book will offer you prayers to pray, declarations to make, affirmations to recite, things to ponder, and ultimately, wisdom and hope to persevere.

Every day is different – just like real life.

Some days we need reminders of how much we are loved. Some days we need reminders to forgive. Some days we need to know that someone is praying for us. So whether you are on top of the mountain or dusting yourself off in the valley, this book will encourage you to keep pressing on day by day.

Often when we find ourselves in a season of weariness, we will also find that a season of transition is upon us. While we may feel as though nothing is happening, nothing is changing, or nothing is moving, the truth is in the midst of our standstill, the Lord is moving and rearranging things on our behalf. However, when we don't see anything happening in the natural, it sometimes becomes too difficult to comprehend that God is truly for us, and consequently, we need a reason to press on.

Made in the USA
San Bernardino, CA
11 December 2018